SINGLE
MOMS

SINGLE MOMS

MAKE YOUR
DREAM A REALITY

GEORGIA ISAAC

Title: Single Mom
Subtitle: Make Your Dream A Reality

ISBN: 978-1-952327-75-9

T.A.L.K. Publishing
5215 North Ironwood Road, Suite 200
Glendale, WI 53217
publishwithtalk.com

CONTENTS

Author's Bio..7

Acknowledgements..9

Introduction 11

Chapter 1   The Dream Versus Reality.............................15

Chapter 2   Becoming A Foster Parent............................25

Chapter 3   Parenting Older Children.............................31

Chapter 4   Coping with Loneliness................................35

Chapter 5   Learn to Let Go and Never Give up 39

Chapter 6   Focus On You and Write Down Your Goals 44

Chapter 7   Prayer Provides Strength 49

Chapter 8   Live for yourself not others..........................53

Chapter 9   Finding Yourself...57

Chapter 10   Laugh, Live, and Love..................................60

Final Thoughts...63

AUTHOR'S BIO

Georgia Isaac was born in Jamaica and moved to the U.S. at the age of twelve. She is the single parent of two biological children and many foster children. Georgia has a bachelor's degree in Social Work and a master's degree in Human Services. She currently works as a care manager with adults with disabilities. Georgia has always had a passion for helping others, particularly children. She hopes to continue to be effective in her community through the encouragement and motivation of others to persevere to achieve their goals.

ACKNOWLEDGEMENTS

I t is important to recognize the people who have come into your life, whether short or long, and let those same people know how much they have impacted your life. To my mother, Rose Brown, thank you for showing me, as a single parent, there is nothing you cannot achieve if you put your mind to it and work hard towards obtaining your goals. For example, watching her work many jobs to make sure her family was taken care of.

Julien Isaac-Carter, my firstborn, thank you for being so patient with me and allowing me to grow as your mother. You taught me how to be a mother, even when we had to learn along the way. Your smile and laughter kept me going daily. You allow me to make mistakes and learn from them. Ethan Walters, you have taught me patience. You keep me on my toes; you consistently challenge me, which only makes me better.

Gregory Isaac, my brother, thank you for always putting aside time from your busy schedule to help with the boys. You did not have to, but you did. You not only made a difference in your nephew's life but in all the foster children that have come into my home. Thank you so much for having such a big heart and being on this journey with me, and for making such a significant impact in so many children's lives in a time when they needed it the most.

Thank you to all the children I have had the opportunity to foster and those I have not had the opportunity to yet. Thank you for giving me a chance to be a part of your life, and I hope my family has helped you along your journey. Genetta Springfield, you and your sons have been such a positive influence on my children. Your children took on a mentoring role to Julien when he really needed big brothers to look up to. Your sons are polite, respectful, responsible, and very patient. As a mother, I know you are so proud of them. Esril Wood (Grandpa), may your soul rest in peace. Thank you so much for always believing in me and trusting me. I was so fortunate to hear your stories and the history of our family and get life lessons. I genuinely enjoyed our Sunday chats. When authoring this book and feeling like giving up, I could hear you say "trouble" you got this; do not give up; I am with you.

Jennifer Daniels, Pamela Sprewer, Acicia Hopf, Carisa DiMattina, Amy Graap, Kyra Appling McCullum, Melanie Randolph, Janet Brown, Junius Brown, Sharina Brown, Rebecca Dyson, Jessica Chmiel, thank you all so much for your love and support.

Sonia Adams, thank you for mentoring/coaching me through this process, your energy and your passion kept me going. You saw my vision and helped me put it into words. I will forever be grateful to you and the TALK team that made this dream a reality.

INTRODUCTION

In life, things happen unexpectedly, and you must adjust your life accordingly. As a child, you imagine what your life will look like when you grow up. As a little girl, you fantasize about your wedding dress, who your husband will be, how many kids you will have, and envision your perfect house.

As an adult, this fantasy often remains in the back of your mind. Everyone is looking for their happily ever after with that special someone. When you meet someone, spend quality time getting to know that someone, and find that you are happy in love, you start to paint a picture of what life would be like for both of you. This feeling of happiness you never want to end. You reflect on when you were a little girl and what you pictured your life would be. Could this be a dream, or is this reality?

Reality sets in when you find out you're pregnant, and your partner's response is that he does not want to have a child. Slowly you start to see your world crumbling in front of your eyes, and this is no longer your dream but your reality. It is hard to believe the same person who professed their love to you could turn their back on you at a time in your life when you thought this was your happily ever after.

The emotional roller-coaster starts; you question the relationship and the moments you spent together leading up to this moment. You find yourself getting angry with the lack of commitment and your trust in someone who you thought was making your dream a reality. How could someone profess their love and make so many promises but leave when he is needed most?

Your new reality now has you starting to question yourself; how I will do this alone, I cannot do this, why me, this is not fair, I do not deserve this, I do not know how to be a mother, how am I going to do this alone?

During those nine months of the pregnancy, emotions are all over the place, either happy, sad, or angry. It is time to hear the baby's heartbeat as you lay there feeling so alone one moment and in the other excited. The nurse looks over with tears running down your cheek, knowing you have a life growing inside of you. A child you are now fully responsible for, the bond between a mother and child begins to build. Over time the bond between the mother and child gets stronger and stronger.

The emotions start again. What are people going to think of me raising a child alone? The body starts to change, weight gain, and weight loss. The day comes when it is time to have the baby. You have someone in your corner that you trust and will support you no matter what. As a first-time mother, you are trying to figure things out along the way. You are not sure if you are doing things right; life just keeps moving. Being a single parent is not something we plan, but it happens. It is up to the person to figure things out along the way and remember we all have good days and bad days. The single parent dream is not something someone wakes up and says to themselves "self, one day I want to be a single parent and raise children on my own." It doesn't mean life doesn't' go on; it just means you have to make an adjustment and be open to suggestions, work on patience, ask for help, and know you're going to have good and bad days.

Instead of making your dream become your reality, make your reality become your dream. It is ok to dream; however, do not allow your dream to blindside your reality. It is easy to focus on the dream and not reality. In a dream, it is a safe place where nothing ever appears to go wrong and things always go right. It is important to hold on to your dream because sometimes those dreams are what hold you together to cope with reality. Sometimes things are not always what they seem. It is important to gather more information to make the best decision. Your thoughts shape your reality. It is important to have a positive thought about yourself. If you do not believe in yourself, how can you expect others to believe in you? It is not easy. If you do not try, you will never know.

This book will journey through my life as a single mom. The good, the bad, and the ugly, my emotions when my dream did not become my reality, how I was able to overcome everything that was put in my way, the steps I had to take, and what I had learned to become the women and mother I am today. My journey on becoming more closer to God and knowing what it truly means to forgive and allow God to lead you on the path he wants you to be on. In life, we wake not knowing what our purpose is, and we keep doing the same thing repeatedly with the same result. It is important to learn something from your day-to-day life, even if it is something exceedingly small.

CHAPTER 1

The Dream Versus Reality

Growing up, I fantasized about life and what it would look like when I grew up, got married, and how many children I would have. I also imagined the colors of my wedding and how my house would look. My dream looked something like this:

> It was such a beautiful wedding seeing two people looking into each other's eyes, professing their love for each other in front of their friends and family. Everyone laughed, smiled, and took pictures with the bride and groom. Everyone noticed the love the spouses had for each other. Next, the spouses go on their honeymoon, which was a wonderful time to spend with someone who shares your dreams and hopes. In a brief time, the spouses buy a house together and over the years are happily in love. During this time, they are both enjoying each other and enjoying being married, and working toward their goals. Before they know it, the wife becomes pregnant,

and the husband shares his excitement and expresses how much he is looking forward to raising a child with his wife. During the nine months, her husband stays at her side to ensure that she and the baby are secure. Once the babies arrive, the father and mother are overjoyed. She is living the life of which she has always dreamed. Sounds splendid! However, as she stepped down from her doorway, a loud noise rang, and it was your alarm clock that woke you up to start your day, and you realized that it was all a dream.

My adult life started when I went off to college in 1997. My dream was to work with children and families, so my focus was on obtaining a degree in Social Work. After four wonderful years in college, I received my bachelor's degree in Social Work in 2001. I then decided to move back to my hometown and pursue a career in social work. My first job was working as a case manager for a Child Welfare System where I worked with children placed in out-of-home care. During this time, I learned to appreciate the insignificant things and be thankful for what I had been blessed to have because on a day-to-day basis, I had seen so many people go without. Because of family struggles and the lack of resources available to individuals, I made it a point on my off days to get as much information from the community to better serve the community, and with this effort, I became the go-to person in the office to provide resources to the community. I believe that if you do not ask, you will never know what you have available to you. It is not easy to ask for help when you are trying to do things on your own, and your pride can step in the way.

In 2005 I was able to purchase my very first home. I had always wanted to own my own home. There is nothing wrong with renting if that is something you want to do, but, for me, it was not something I wanted so I decided to purchase my home. The search to locate my home during this time had me driving around the area I wished to live in and search for sale signs. When I came upon the house I would later purchase, I fell in love with it right away. There was a lady looking out the window and when she saw me, she asked if I wanted to see the house. As she walked me around the home it was small, but when she took me into the backyard, I could see myself sitting in the backyard drinking a glass of wine and just relaxing. There is nothing like having your own home and being able to come and go without any on complaining about music, lights, or who you have coming over to your home. I knew what I wanted, and I was going to take the necessary steps to purchase this house. A week later I was informed that I was denied because my credit was too low. I then contacted the same relator I worked with at the time and told her about the house and my visit with the current owner. My realtor took over and worked her magic and I was able to purchase my first home. I remember my first night in the home, I was full of emotions due to the prior owner leaving everything in the house. It was as if they were running from something or someone. I decided to make a few calls to agencies that I worked with asking if they needed clothes, future, and other items for individuals who were homeless, or in shelter.

In 2005 I met a man who I thought I was going to spend the rest of my life with. The relationship started so great. We spent so much time getting to know each other, our likes, and dislikes. You know how when you first meet someone you spend every hour on the phone talking all night. The thought of being in a relationship with someone who adores you and talks about the future. During this time nothing could go wrong in life, everything was going great; new house, new man, and then I find out I was pregnant, and this came as a shock. I remember walking around the house saying to myself, is this real. So back to the store I go to buy more pregnancy tests just to make sure I was seeing what I was seeing. After taking more tests I decided to make a doctor's appointment to confirm again what I had saw. Once I received the confirmation from the doctor, it was time to tell the father the good news. Or what I saw as good news since being able to carry a life is such a blessing because not many people are able to do so. The good news was not good news for the father as when he received the news he walked away and never looked back not matter how many times I tried to engage him. This was the moment when my life started as a single parent.

On an evening in 2006, I went into labor. I called my friend to take me to the hospital. During the labor I sat waiting to give birth to my first child with no father around to support and encourage and love on me during this special time. When it was time to bring my firstborn home, I walked into an empty house with no one to welcome us home. During this time, I had to reply on my friends for support. The late-night feeding and the pumping during the day and at night. I found myself doing the same routine over and over. The difficulty with not having enough money to cover all the bills and having to make payment arrangement with creditors to ensure things did not get cut off due to the lack of payments.

The second time around being a single parent was different as I was in a much longer relationship. The feeling of making plans to spend the rest of my life with this person brings so much excitement. The feeling of happiness kicked in as this person made a commitment to spend the rest of his life with me. I started telling everyone the good news and over time started sitting down to make plan towards a wedding and during this time I became pregnant. It felt so good to have a man at my side cheering me on to bring our child into this world. Over time things change. Due to a woman's intuition, the marriage never happened and the relationship ended due to infidelity.

During this time, I was out of work and needed additional assistance. I will never forget the day I went to apply for government assistance. The young lady that was assigned to meet with me that day looked me in the eyes and said, "you do not qualify for assistance due to your educational background". She said I was overqualified and wanted to know why I had a problem locating employment. I remember walking out of the building so angry. I am a taxpayer and I have never asked for extra help. But when I did, the system turned on me. A mother with, now, two children and no income. This is a time when I had to put my pride aside and locate pantries and other community resources to continue to provide for my children. As an already single parent, I knew what I needed to do. I spent days and days looking and was finally able to locate employment, however the cost of daycare was more than what I was getting paid on the job. Through a friend I was able to locate an affordable childcare provider and she turned out to be so supportive. "I will never leave you nor forsake you." Hebrews 13:5.

In becoming a single parent of two beautiful boys in 2006 and again in 2013. This was not the dream I had planned for myself or my children; however, I adjusted to what my life had become. The feelings of loneliness and uncertainty often juggled through my mind as I continued to parent. Like my mother, and many of my peers who also came from single-family homes, and as a child, you do not think much about it other than "it is normal". As you get older, you notice other families have two parents and you wonder what happened to yours but never ask questions. It is not easy for a parent to explain why the other parent decided not to be involved in the children's life. When you do not have the answer yourself, as a parent, you do your best to ensure your child is always loved and cared for, which I do daily. I am involved with everything that pertains to my boys, and there are many good days and bad days, but the good outweighs the bad.

As a first-time single parent, you do not know what you are doing most of the time you guess and figure things out along the way. Sometimes, I would find myself reading books for the answers to my questions. Additionally, I gained insight from my friends who have had children. There were times when I would be so exhausted and did not have anyone to watch the boys for a few minutes to allow me to recharge. As I learned to adjust my schedule and take increased breaks to allow myself to breathe, I had to learn to put some things off for another day and time. It was challenging and time-consuming, so I had to make a lot of sacrifices and put aside my own needs to make sure my children's needs were met. As a result, there were a lot of sleepless nights and times when I would worry about how I was going to put food on the table. I never stop working hard so I could ensure my children never go without. It is with God's grace and a lot of praying I was able to make things happen. There were times when the kids wanted to sign up for an activity and I did not have the money. I learned to become creative and we found other things to do. Over time, I learned how to bake and have bake sales, rummage sales, and anything the kids could get involved in to help and learn at the same time.

Through all these struggles, I realized I am a great cook and a decent baker. As a single parent, you will see your true support system. If you are like me, growing up you were always willing to lend a helping hand. Everyone knew they could count on you in their time of need. The biggest challenges are when the table is turned and you are in need of some help and no one is to be found. This has never stopped me from going after what I want. I never stopped working hard to put forth the effort needed to ensure my children have what they need.

Sometimes when people are looking in, they are not aware of the struggles; all they see is the outcome. It is so important to check on others even if they appear to the be the strongest ones in the group. You never know what is truly going on unless you ask.

My mother was also a single parent, and she did everything possible to provide for us. She made sure her kids do not want anything, showed us we must work hard to get what we need and want and when we get it, learn to appreciate it, and never forget how hard you worked to get. I relied a lot on my community resources. She located a lot of programs that were free in the community. We attended them, we went to the park, and we did everything to enjoy each other's company.

During that time, I also gotten my master's degree in Human Services. It was not easy, but I knew I had to show my children that when you start something, you must finish it. I started that program with my firstborn because I struggled so much that year, I put my masters on hold; however, I went back to school and finished many years later. I never want my children to see me start something and not finish.

As stated previously, single parenting does not mean life is over. It means large tasks are ahead, which will only make you stronger. There will be times of sadness, happiness, fun, laughter, focus, anger, disappointment, crying, joy, and a feeling of accomplishment. As a parent, we are our children's first role model, so it is important to set the tone for the children. It is essential to take away all distractions, watch the children, and see some of the things they do that they noticed by watching the parent's habits. One day, one of my children held the door open for people to enter, and a lady came to tears and said, "you're doing such a wonderful job with the boy's". It is not very often I see kids with such kind and loving hearts, and at that moment, overwhelming joy will come upon the parent. As a parent, it is important to let the children know when we are proud of them. As a parent, you cannot hold on to the anger of having to raise children on your own when it was not the dream you had for yourself.

Instead of making your dream become your reality, make your reality become your dream. It is ok to dream however, do not allow your dream to blindside your reality. It is easy to focus on the dream and not reality. In a dream there is a safe place where nothing ever appears to go wrong, and something is always going right. It is important to hold on to your dream because sometimes those dreams are what hold you together to cope with reality. Things may always seem to go wrong but if you change your mindset, you will start to see more positive than negative. and when the negative arises you will look at it as a steppingstone towards whatever it is that you are working toward in the moment. Have you never noticed in life you have positives and negatives? Think of batteries, you have positive side and a negative side. Without one or the other it will not work. Look at the many things we need batteries for in life; weather radios, pedometers, fitness trackers, alarm clocks, cameras, doorbells, home appliances, toys, games, and cordless tools. This list could go on and on. We will have positives and negatives. When you focus on the negative you never have time to see the positive going on in your life. Your thoughts shape your reality. It is important to have positive thoughts about yourself. If you do not believe in yourself, how can you expect others to believe in you? How will you ever know you are good at something if you never try.

CHAPTER 2

Becoming A Foster Parent

In life you never know where your journey will lead you and what it is you will see along that journey. You will come across several paths in life, and you may often be unsure of which path you should take. If you never choose a path, you will never know the outcome. As a single parent we must make decisions daily, and sometimes those decisions can often be right and often be wrong, but if you do not decide, you will never know the outcome and you will always wonder.

It is not easy to raise children on your own and much harder raising children who are not biologically yours. Over the years of working in the child welfare system with children who have been placed in out-of-home care, I have observed many children aging out of the system with the lack of basic life skills needed to thrive in this world. This has made me incredibly sad as a single parent and I knew how hard it was to be on your own and not have all the support systems in place to ensure your needs are being met.

In my experiences in working with teenagers who are placed in out of home care, its often difficult to locate homes willing to take these children in. This continues to be an ongoing issue. As a single parent I have taken on this task. It is so important to find a balance and when the time is right making a decision that is best for you and your family. Many people find it difficult to take in teens when they are often dealing with self-esteem and body image, defiant behaviors, peer-pressure, and competitions and as a single parent this can be overwhelming to handle alone. Image if everyone gave up on you and you had no choice but to figure things out on your own. Learning how to do things on your own is what a single parent must do when the other parent decides to leave. I cannot imagine for a teenager what it would be like to have both parents give up on their responsibilities.

Many of the teens have I worked with have stated that people will say they love and trust you however, when times get hard the person decides they are no longer wanting you in their home. As a parent we teach our children life skills. Children who are in out-of-home care struggle with stability which can lead to some kids getting lost along the way.

I remember a time when I sat with a few kids to fill out job applications and noticed that many of them did not know how to fill the application out. I took it upon myself to meet with a few of my teens at local restaurant to assist them with filling out application and how to speak with a manger. As we all sat there the manger spoke with each teen individually. For these kids not having the ability to fill out an application or even the process of what it entailed to be a part of a job interview, it took so much of me to hold back the tears knowing these teens where a few months away from no longer being in the system, out in the world on their own and they did not know how to read or write. During this time I decided I wanted to become a foster parent and make a difference. Unfortunately this was not an option at the time due to a conflict of interest with my employment. This feeling of wanting to do more stayed with me for a long time. When I started working with adults with disabilities is when I started the process of becoming a foster parent. I decided to talk to my older son prior to taking the next steps. I sat my son down and explained to him what it meant to be a foster parent. I explained what it meant when children are placed in out-of-home care and his response was, "mommy if kids need help let us help them." Even though I already had so much going on, I decided to become a Treatment Foster Parent.

The official decision started making negative thoughts rise again; you cannot do this this, you do not have enough money, people will talk about you being a single parent with so many kids, you are not going to always get approval. Do not allow the negative thoughts to take over now, know what your goals are, how important they are to you and start working towards them. I knew what I wanted to do, the changes I wanted to make, and the difference I wanted to see in the all the children we encountered.

Knowing you have taken the first step towards becoming foster parents is so important. During the process of becoming a foster parent, there are classes and training that are needed to get licensed. A home study involves background checks for everyone who lives in the home, home visits, financial statements, educations, employment, and references.

When fostering, it is important to connect with an agency who is supportive and will support the needs of the children placed in out-of-home are being met. Once you have decided on an agency it is important to check their website to see if it offers a brief introduction video or a question & answer video or session. Thereafter filling out an application and start the process. My licensing agency provided childcare during the training; The children looked forward to going to the daycare while I attended my trainings. The boys looked forward to meeting new people and making new friends. I have had the opportunity to foster so many children. Recently, I was able to assist a young man that had been placed in my home for five years. He graduated from high school and went off to college. I went from being a parent of two to a parent of five, it was not easy, but we made things happen every day. I give God thanks for allowing me to have the strength the wisdom, and support of my siblings.

There are moments as a foster parent when you do not have the answers. The time your foster child comes to and asks, "how come my parents did not want me and how come your family treats me better than my own family?" The most awkward thing to explain to a child when you truly do not know the answer "is take the time to find the answer". I should say the best answer but really there is no best answer for a parent not wanting to take responsibility for their child anymore. Fostering has taught my children how to appreciate their mother and everything and everyone that comes their way. My brother Greg decided to come along this journey with me of fostering, and what I mean by that is he became the person I call when I need a break and in doing so, a lot of the boys that I foster grew attached to him and looked to him as the support.

Children pay attention to everything you do, everything you say. Over the years I have fostered so many children. Being able to spend time with other children and provide them with the guidance and support they need in a most critical time of their life has been such a reward. It is so rewarding to see the look on your child's face when they know you are their biggest fan. I have experienced times when my child was playing sports and other kids have their father's around cheering them on, the pain in a child's face from not having a father to cheer him on is the most hurtful thing to ever see. These are the moments you turn up the volume and you become the loudest fan in the room. This can also change the room and everyone else in it the other parents start to cheer for your child. In these moments the child knew mom was going to do anything possible to take away the pain.

This is the same for my foster children. We may not look alike, however, the child knows he has someone in the audience cheering and rooting for him to succeed. It does not mean you have to look like me for us to be family. It is important to remember every child has a different story and no child is alike, sometimes what you try for one child will not work for the other.

I am sure like everyone we all grew up being compared to other relatives and you would always say to yourself I am nothing like them. It was not that your parent or family wanted you to be like that person, they saw a quality in the induvial they felt you could have inherited. It is important to allow your children to figure out who they are. We cannot compare others to them. It is important to know that what may have worked in the past may not work now in the present. Things are always revolving and adjusting and it only betters your relationship with your children.

In this world, children have so many distractions and more opportunities available to them. The world has changed and if we do not change with it, we will be lost and unable to communicate with our children. We are not going to be able to relate to what they are dealing or coping with. We live in a world where the internet provides us with so many resources. As a parent it so important to utilize the resources available to assist with parenting and understanding some of the thing's kids are now dealing with in school and in the community. Fostering is not easy, however, if you stay committed and open to suggestions, things become easier as time passes. Be strong, and let your heart take courage, all you who wait for the Lord! Psalm 31:24

CHAPTER 3

Parenting Older Children

As children get older, they look for more guidance from the parent. There are times when the kids feel they no longer need the guidance from the parent and feel they can do things on their own. Sometimes there are days and nights when it feels like everything is going wrong and it gives an overwhelming feeling of am I doing this right or am I messing up my kid's life. Days when it feels like the children are working your nerves and days when the parent is full of joy. Moments when one of your children brings home something they made from school, wants you to have it, and you act like it is the best gift you have ever received. You are going to have nights that you do not get a lot of sleep. There are nights when your baby just keeps crying and you do not know what is going on and the reason he or she is crying. It can be frustrating not knowing the reason your baby is crying when you have tried everything: clean diaper, feeding, story time, walking around and you just cannot put your finger on it.

As the children get older you learn to cope with the different emotions they go through. It is not easy for your child to figure out who they are and where they fit in life. Sometimes, they take their feelings and frustrations out on you, and it is not that they do not care, they are having a tough time themselves with what is going on with them. And no one is around to say you are doing such an excellent job or to notice your tough times it is hard. Having to tell yourself all the time you are doing an amazing job and keep it up helps. Learn to praise yourself first and appreciate being you, even though having the kids say thank you or they appreciate you would make the day. Sometimes things happen when you least expect it. Days when it seems like nothing is going right try to focus by standing still for a few minutes, even if it is in the bathroom. Allow yourself some quiet time to pull yourself together.

Now in life you must stay focused and become highly creative with kids who have a short attention span. It can be so frustrating and stressful around the house when everyone is doing their own thing and everyone loses track of what is profoundly important. To interact with the children becoming creative helps. Something that works is making flashcards with questions. I've made cards with what's your favorite color, who is your favorite music artist, if you could travel anywhere in the world where it would be, if you could drive any vehicle what it would be, what is your favorite vacation trip that we took and why or you could ask what vacation trip you would like to take and why. The point of the cards is to get everyone talking and soon you will no longer need the cards. Sometimes this works for my family; it may not work for you it but does not hurt to try.

Having more than one child means different interests. You must learn to balance everything which can be so overwhelming. The sky is not the limit so there's no limit being a single parent is not what you dreamed or planned for yourself, but we all have dreams, and we all have plans. Sometimes things do not work out as we planned to make the best of it and going in with a positive attitude there's going to be obstacles in the way of getting things accomplish.

As stated previously single parenting does not mean life is over, it means large tasks are ahead which will only make you stronger. There are times of sadness, happiness, fun, laughter, focus, anger, disappointments, crying, joy, and a feeling of accomplishment. As a parent, we are our children first role model children see adults it is important to set the tone for the children. It is important to take away all distractions, watch the children, and see some of the things they do the thing they noticed by watching the parent's habits. One day one of the children during one of our outings held the door open for people to enter and leave the store. A lady came to tears and said you are doing such an excellent job with the boys. It is not very often I see kids with such kind and loving hearts. In that moment overwhelming joy came upon the parents. As a parent it is important to let the children know when we are proud of them. One of the most important things I feel when parenting older children is being open to not just them learning from you, but you learning form them as well. We are never too young or never too old to learn something new. I have noticed when I allow myself to lean from my children, they are more open to come and talk to me and they are more willing to share tough times in their lives and we are able to work through things. As a parent we must realize children are going through more distractions than we as parent never had. We have to learn to adapt and lean and teach our children how to not allow all these distractions to turn them away from the bigger picture, whatever that picture may be. Proverbs 22:6 KJV states train up a child in the way he would go; and when he is older, he will not depart from it.

CHAPTER 4

Coping with Loneliness

In life we all have found ourselves coping with loneliness at some point in our lives. What does it really mean to be lonely? Well according to dictionary, loneliness means sadness because one has no friends or company. One of the greatest feelings we could ever have is feeling connected. Being able to connect through, love, ideas, and friends when you agree or even disagree with someone is helpful. Everyone has experienced a time when they were lonely in their life. During the pandemic everyone was forced to stay in their homes and during this time most people were faced with isolation, which can be so painful just feeling disconnected from the world. So many people struggled with not having someone to talk to during the pandemic. Not being able to talk to people at the park, dog park, or passing a person in the store can make you feel alone.

As a parent you are always making sure everyone elses needs are met when one question comes up. At times you will sit in your room and cry and feel sorry for yourself and that is ok if you do not allow yourself to remain in that feeling for an exceptionally long time. Don't look for someone to fill your loneliness unless that is what you're looking for. Loneliness is temporary and will not last always. It may seem like it, but it does not allow yourself time to remain in this situation for everyone. Have you ever found yourself thinking about everyone in your life such as friends and family and say to yourself "why does everyone around me seem so happy?" Sometimes we see others and they seem to be doing so well in in their lives. We sometimes look at our own life and say to ourselves "why can't that be me?" You must remember, just because everything seems happy on the outside does not mean they are on the inside.

As a single parent, there will be times when you feel comfortable with wanting to start dating, take it slow, take it slow. You want to be able to get to know somebody, know their true intentions. You also want to take a chance so do not be afraid to take a chance because you never know what the outcome may be.

I have learned if you stay busy you keep your mind from wondering and when I say wondering it means keeping the negative thoughts away. You know sometimes in life there is so much negativity around you, but do not allow that negativity through your mind. Try to stay positive and know that whatever is coming, whoever is coming, you deserve the best, nothing less! Thinking of dating while being a single mom can be difficult to explain to someone that has never been in your position, but it's OK to feel happy, it's OK to want to spend some time with another adult, it is OK and tell yourself it's OK. It's OK to dress up however you feel comfortable and it's OK to feel good, get your hair done, nails done, or just put on that outfit that you've been longing to put on.

Do whatever it is that makes you feel comfortable cause when you are comfortable that's when amazing things start to . happen, you have more joy in your life. For the ones who do not feel dating is something that they need to do, continuing doing whatever it is that makes you happy, just make sure you not dwelling in the loneliness. I know sometimes as single parents we pretend nothing bothers us and underneath we are in so much pain. Believe, pray, and talk to God, talk to whoever it is that you feel is your higher power. I spend a lot of my time talking to God because he doesn't judge me. He listens to me, and I always hear, "keep praying I hear you be patient." I know you are saying to yourself it has been years I feel like I have been patient. But guess what? You know when you bake something sometimes you may not get it right the first time, so you must keep trying and keep trying until you've perfected the way.

Do not compare your life to anyone else because you never know what that person is dealing with in their own personal life. The person you are thinking about might be wishing they had your life. Take this time to get to know yourself. You cannot ask someone to love you when you are not loving yourself. When you start motivating yourself things will start changing around you. Start saying "I am a great parent, I am beautiful, I am happy, I am strong, I am a great mother, I am loveable, I am who I am, I am somebody, I am relentless, I am special, I am phenomenal, I am here to show you anything is possible."

Do not wait for someone to push you towards your goals. Learn to love the process that you're taking towards your goal. Do the work even when no one is watching. It is so easy to give up when times get hard, we all need a little encouragement sometimes to keep pushing forward. It is different when you do not have someone to say keep going you can do it. That is when you truly must look deep within yourself and push yourself. Psalm 42:8 says the Lord will command his loving kindness in the daytime; and his son will be with me in the night.

CHAPTER 5

Learn to Let Go and Never Give up

Life never seems to go as planned, and when it does not we tend to focus on the negative. We focus so much energy on the negative that we forget what it is like to feel happiness or joy. Learning to forgive is not easy and it takes time, but you must be open to forgive. Knowing your dream is not your reality does not mean your reality could not be your dream. Never let go of your dream and never give up on the love that you see for yourself. When you harbor so much anger, it blinds you from your blessings. The more you hold on to anger, the more you lose a good piece of you. The more you hold on to the hurt you are not allowing yourself to live. It is so easy to hold on to the hurt and hard to let go.

Learn to forgive yourself and once this forgiveness starts you will too. When you learn to do this thing, God will open your eyes to so many things. When you learn to forgive a person who has done you wrong, it is takes a load off your chest. It is not easy, but you must really, I mean really think about it. Why are you holding on to the pain? You are holding on to the pain and the person has moved on. I was angry for so long that I started to lose myself until one day I stood in my living room crying and shouted aloud to God, "I need you and I do not want to be in pain anymore teach me how to forgive." That same year I learned the importance of forgiving and I started to allow myself to start living and enjoying every moment with my children. It is so important to not have anyone hold anything over you. When you allow God to show you the way it is such an amazing feeling. I am not perfect in God's eyes. You are going to make mistakes daily and that is ok. Learn to let go of your past mistakes because holding on to them will only hold you back. Learn from your mistakes and move forward. If we hold on to things we cannot change.

Learning to never give up is so hard in life. Taking the effortless way out is safe and convenient. Have you ever committed to something and when it got hard you gave up because of the pain that you were feeling, the guilt of am, "I not trying hard enough."? Have you ever started something and just quit in your mind, telling yourself, "it is too hard, I cannot do it is impossible, I'm not going to win anyways."? Have you ever sat down and told yourself, "do not give up never give up."? Sometimes you have to be your biggest motivator when there is nobody else around. You must cheer you on!

When you give up on things it becomes a habit, one of the greatest feelings is being able to stick something out to the end. You end up feeling so overwhelmed with joy, just so many emotions because you worked hard at something and finished it. You made it through some bumps and things that came in the way along the way, but you pushed it out of the way, moved it and jumped over it, and did everything possible to obtain whatever it is that you were trying to accomplish.

This is the same thing with parenting, there are so many things that may end up in the middle of the road but along the way you must find ways to move those things to continue to move forward. It is not always easy, you are going to sweat, you will have bumps and bruises and you are going to get scars, but you never give up! If you give up, your child will see you give up and they may give up. Do not give up on you or your children. You are not alone even if it sometimes feels that way. Tomorrow is always a new day to try again. Take a first and then a second breath, not a short breath, take a deep breath and hold it in. Hear yourself breathing in and out, allow yourself to just relax.

In life I had to decide to no longer complain about the things that were not going the way I wanted them to go. I had to change my mindset and start looking at the positive and start working off them. Sometimes we can become a little lazy and stop working on our dreams. It is important to not give up and allow yourself to continue to grow and realize there are going to be challenges along the way. You must work even harder when times get tough, being negative will not allow you to grow it only keeps you at a standstill.

I had to come to a point in my life when I became sick and tired of doing the same thing over and over and not feel like I was making a difference. I came to a point in my life when I realized God was continuing to test me, to see if I was ready for purpose in life. It was not easy along the way, but I was willing to take a chance on myself and not allow myself to not be afraid to succeed.

When I started noticing other single mothers struggling with the of lack resources needed to maintain daily, I realized I did not have it all bad and I wanted to make a difference and assist other single mothers with identifying resources. It is not easy being a single parent and when you feel you do not have the support you need and the lack of resources, a person must decide if this is going to hold them back or use it to motivate you to move forward. I never allowed myself to get complacent. I had to figure out what I needed to do for me to grow and move forward. Sometimes God will move a people from your life for you to move forward, people can hold you back from what your true purpose. God will add and remove people from your life to allow you to grow. Have your ever noticed when a person is removed from your life that person will sometimes stay on your mind. This is God's way of saying this person will return in your life again later.

To elevate you must have patience as you get closer to what your what you are trying to achieve. The most important thing to do is change your mindset and never give up. You must understand that times in life circumstances in your life will try to get you to give up, but do not.

"Be strong, and let your heart take courage, all you who wait for the Lord." Psalm 31:24.

When you find peace in your life, things become clean and you get a better understanding on life and what it has to offer. People start to notice your change and wonder what happened in your life that cause you to change. Some may like the change and other's may not. Make changes for yourself not for others. I had to make changes in my life to grow into the woman I am today. I had to learn to let go of the past, the anger, and never give up on myself. This was not easy; however, I knew I had to make some changes because if I continued live my life with anger, I would continue to block my blessings. God has blessed me in allowing me to find myself and love the woman I have become through everything my kids and I had to endure.

Ecclesiastes 9:11 says, "I returned, and saw under the sun, that the race is not to the swift, nor the battle to the strong, neither yet bread to the wise, nor yet riches to men of understanding, nor yet favour to men of skill; but time and chance happeneth to them all."

CHAPTER 6

Focus On You and Write Down Your Goals

Single parents tend to focus on everyone else but themselves. It is important to remember we have an extraordinary capability. It is important to try and figure out what it is that you are good at. Your gift is something you do not have to put a lot of effort into it. It is important to start writing down your goals. What type of things do you want to accomplish. Having kids does not mean you are not able to accomplish dreams. Sometimes, some goals are put on hold; you must start working on others in the meantime. Get a notebook and place it at the side of your bed and when an idea comes to mind just write it down. Start off by trying to write down one goal per night. It can be something small like I want to start making the bed daily, it does not matter what it is, just start. You are not going to be able to write a goal every night because some nights are going to be crazier than other nights. What do you do when do you accomplish your goals? You can make family goals and celebrate together. It is important to post goals where you can see them.

We can take care of our kids and take care of ourselves as well. Have faith in God and have faith in yourself. Make sure you are mindful of who you share your goals with. Not everyone has your best interest at heart and not everyone is meant to be on your journey with you. Do not let anyone ever let you feel like you are not able to be a parent and work on your goals as well. You are going to have people talking saying you have taken time away from your children and that is not true. Do what is best for you and your children. You are no good for your children if you are always walking around the home angry. Show your children, the sky is not the limit. No matter what they put their minds and heart to, they can accomplish them with hard work and commitment.

You can do an activity with your kids and have them write down their goals also. This can be a family activity. No one is alone in their journey. Another way to accomplish this is you can make poster boards so they can visualize their goals. I get a lot of the magazines, glue sticks, scissors, pens, crayons, markers, whatever and I call it no "TV Day" and we focus on our goals.

They can then put their boards wherever they can use them for motivation. Maybe post them all in the kitchen for all to see so you can hold each other accountable. Whenever someone accomplishes, a goal be it big or small, celebrate, show them that they should never feel that they cannot reach for the stars.   As single mothers we often find ourselves taking care of everyone but ourselves. We forget to laugh, smile, and enjoy life. It is ok to be there for everyone but never, forget who you are. I know it feels so good when you look around and everyone is happy, I know deep down you are not always happy, you feel tired sometimes, you do not always feel sexy, and you are lacking sleep. Learn to love you again, find likes and dislikes they may not be the same prior to you having children but those likes still make you happy. Take time to watch a TV series with your favorite drink, or go to a movie, even if its alone, do not ever be afraid to go alone. Sometimes you need time alone to just relax. If movies are not your thing, get your hair done or nails done, or go to your local bookstore and take an hour to just read your favorite book. You do not have to do things that cost money. You can just sit at home and do anything that brings you joy. You can see if your girlfriends are up to coming over and just chill. If you enjoy cooking or baking, you can bake yourself something special. When you are doing any of these things try not to feel guilty for taking care of yourself.

In life we focus so much on what others think we must stop, we have too many other things going on in our life. When you find time for yourself, you can recharge yourself. You know when you start a relationship, you are trying to make the best impression, which is the same thing as motherhood. As a first-time mother you are trying to make that good impression you do not want to mess up, you want to make sure that your child is good.

I know everybody can remember the first time somebody asked to hold your child you are like "did you wash your hands?"

When that second child comes, and somebody asks you can I hold the baby, you are often going to just hand the baby over. This does not mean you are a bad parent it just means you have learned from your first child and with the second you are much calmer. You are more aware, you are more educated on things.

The same holds true for a relationship. You know how you can sometimes lose yourself because you are so busy trying to make sure the person you are interested in, or you love sees the best in you? You must remember to not lose yourself along the way trying to impress people and making sure others are always happy.

There was a time that I forgot about myself. We were scheduled to take a trip to see my grandfather in Kentucky, I packed everybody's clothes including my significant others at the time and upon reaching Kentucky realizing I did not pack any clothes for myself. I had to go to the nearest store and buy myself a few things to get by. This is how easy it can be to forget about yourself because your focus is always on others.

It is okay to make sure you pack your stuff first before you pack everyone else's, it is OK to treat yourself sometimes, it is OK to feel selfish sometimes you deserve it, it is OK to just want to lay around sometimes and watch a movie, read a book, and go for walk. It is OK to just want to sit in silence, it is OK to have a glass of wine, it's OK to have your favorite cup of ice cream, it's OK to drink a couple of your favorite teas, it's OK if you just want to take a nap, and it's OK if you want to just take a weekend to yourself. If you do not have supports in place who can watch the kids for a night, then take advantage of that quiet time when the kids go to sleep. Sometimes we forget to take advantage of the simplest time.

CHAPTER 7

Prayer Provides Strength

Growing up as kids we would often watch awards shows and would notice the winners would say thank you and I could not do this without you. We would laugh not knowing what the true meaning of "thank you God". I never truly knew how to pray until I became older, and I learned it on my own. It took me many years to fully understand what it meant to truly pray. As a single parent my faith has been constantly evaluated and I needed something or someone to honestly believe in and to believe in me. Growing up I was taught to believe in God, but I never took that time to figure out what that truly meant.

Over the years I attended church services. I became closer to God through my journey of being a single parent. When times get hard, I would sit and pray and ask for guidance and support and help to get though the tough times and celebrate the good times. When things seem like they are never going to get better I would pray and pray and pray and learned to be patient. When things did not seem to change is when I started to give up hope and my patience is the only thing that kept me going. I also had to learn that prayer meant practice for you to get better at it.

The more I put my faith and trust in God, he started to bring the right people into my life and removed the people who did not mean me well. I became more confident in myself and I started to see myself in a different eye. I started praying before I did everything, and I noticed I had more confidence in myself the more I continued to pray. The more I prayed the more weight started to lift off my body and I felt lighter and lighter. I had to learn to provide my children with an emotional safe place. Psalm 66:19, "But truly God has listened; he has attended to the voice of my prayer."

I started to believe that all things are possible when I believe in God and myself. When I started believing, things started happening. Have your ever drove on the same road home all the time and you would come to an intersection and notice another road but your never took that road, you just wonder where does it lead? Until one day you decided to take that other road and notice that road was much shorter than you one you have been taking all along. You then start asking yourself why you never went down that road before. I could have been saving myself some time. It was not your time to go down that road until that moment and since taking that little chance you are now seeing changes. Sometimes the little steps move your forward to the bigger outcome.

I recently noticed God has always been in control, and he continues to be in control of my life. When I look back on so many times in my life when I did not think I was ready to do something, he would push me or move a situation around so that I could tackle the situation when I was ready. People are always looking in from the outside not truly knowing what is happing on the inside. Luke chapter 10:27-34. "You shall love the Lord your God with all your heart and with all your soul and with all your strength and with all your mind, and your neighbor as yourself." And he said to him, "You have answered correctly; do this, and your will live." By he, desiring to justify himself said to Jesus, "and who is my neighbor?' Jesus replied, "A man was going down the Jerusalem to Jericho, and he fell among robber, who stripped him, beat him, and departed, leaving him half dead. "Now by chance a priest was going down the road, and when he saw him, he passed by on the other side. So likewise, a Levite, when he came to the place and tell him; passed by on the other side. "But a Samaritan, as journeyed came to where he was, and when he saw him, he had compassion. "He went to him and bond up his wounds, pouring on oil and wine. Then he set him on his own animal and brough him to an inn and took care of him. In life we never know who will truly be there when you really need them. It will not always be your family, sometimes it will be stranger who become family. I grew up saying the following prayer: Our Father, who art in heaven hallowed by thy name, thy kingdom come, thy will be done on earth as it is in heaven. Give us this day our daily bread and forgiven us our trespasses, as we forgive those who trespass against us and lead us not into temptation but deliver us from evil for thine is the kingdom, the power, and the glory, forever and ever. Amen!

Sometimes the way things will change in life is through prayer. Prayer is the simplest thing to do. It is you having a conversation with God. It is crazy how the only time we pray is when we need something. When I started praying through the good and tough times is when things started changing, things became clearer. I pray several times per day and it has helped get me through the day. I was not just praying. I started believing in the prayers and having faith that God was hearing my prayers. When times were not going so well, and I had no one to turn to, I started praying more because I had someone who was not passing judgment. It is such a great feeling to be able to feel so free.

CHAPTER 8

Live for yourself not others

In life we tend to focus on everyone else and forget about ourselves. We are so fixated on making sure that everyone has what they need, when they need it. Have you ever catered a party inside your home? You make sure the house is clean, the food is prepared, everyone has something to drink, and afterwards you clean up before you realize that you never made sure you ate or had something to drink? There comes a time in life when you have to say enough is enough, I must put me first for me to be able to not live a miserable life. I was so focused on making sure everyone was taken care of that I forgot about me.

Growing up I focused on what others thought about me instead of what I thought about myself. I learned to change because I want to change not because of what others wanted. Sometimes we must challenge ourselves to learn to deeply appreciate who we truly are. Learn to challenge yourself to be better and learn to forgive yourself. I had to learn to forgive myself and understand that in life I am going to make mistakes and for me to grow I have to learn from the mistakes I make. In life I thought making a mistake was a terrible thing. I have learned it is not a terrible thing and to teach my children that making a mistake is not bad, it is what helps you grow and understand yourself. In life mistakes are going to happen, what matters is how you manage the mistakes that will determine how you move forward. When you become a parent, everyone has their own input – Don't let people judge you, people keep you in a bubble, they will not always support or affirm you. Let God affirm and not people. We humans are the most difficult species, especially the world of now. People will try to lead you through their own way or perspective on how things should be. Live for yourself regardless of the options of others. When you start living for yourself you will find less, and less people want to be around you because the attention is no longer on them. When you start living a life you love and a life you are proud of, it makes your world much easier t. Live for yourself means just be happy. When one door closes another door opens but sometimes, we focus on the reason the first door closed and never pay attention to the door that is open and the opportunities awaiting. It is so important to learn more about yourself, what are you likes and dislikes. Learn to appreciate yourself the good and the bad. I have noticed, in life people will pretend they are happy for you, however deep down they are hoping you are going to fail. I remember a time in college when a professor once said to me, she did not know the reason I am going into the field of social work when she knows I am not going to make it. It is crazy how a person can have a negative impact on your dream. I never allowed what this person said stop me from working towards my goals. It forced me to work harder for myself and the people I had plan to make an impact on. Life is exceedingly difficult when you are so busy trying to live for everyone else. When you know who you are, no one's opinions can stop you!

Growing up I was taught to study hard, get good grades, and go to college to find a job to pay the bills. I have tried different things, different careers, and different roles, but no matter what changed I still did not feel fulfilled. This does not mean I was unhappy with the career opportunities I had, it just means God had bigger purposes for me and they were not clear to me yet. When I started living my life for me and not others is when I became happy with who I am. I stopped allowing fear to take over my life. The fear of running out of money and fear of failure or what other people would think. I truly started figuring out what my fears were and telling myself the truth,my fears were not real and finding the courage to move pass them My first time doing so was when I was interviewed on TV for The Boys & Girls Club. After turning down this opportunity twice already, the third time I prayed, and God said yes without me knowing this would be my first step towards changing my life. Before I walked out in front of the cameras, I prayed and asked God to fill my mouth with the words he wanted his people to hear because it was not about me, it was about the message. After this event I felt so empowered like nothing could stand in my way. The fear of what other people think will no longer have such a strong hold on me. I began to fill my life with joy and happiness and surrounded myself with people who motivated me and pushed me to better. I must come to a decision that the only thing that matters is what I think of myself. I spend time with myself to learn more about myself and in doing so I receive guidance on how to move forward and how to solve my programs and realize what my dreams are.

CHAPTER 9

Finding Yourself

In chapter 4, I spoke about coping with loneliness. During the pandemic we all had to face loneliness and I had to truly get to know myself. This time allowed me to have more conversations with God and ask Him to show me my purpose. I know I am not the only one that has felt so confused at one point in their life and did not know if I was fulfilling my true purpose. I have always felt I was created for something bigger and each day I struggle with not knowing what that may be. The more I have faith and ask God for guidance, I get a better understanding of what it is that I am supposed to be doing.

To utterly understand your purpose, you must understand your fears and anxiety, and not allow them to overcome you. For you to truly connect with a person, first you must know who you are so when you do get the chance to connect with a person, we should take this time to truly get to know our self and when you start connecting with people again you will be a fuller person. When you are a single parent you focus all your time and energy on your children you forget how being yourself again and how to allow someone to truly get to know you.

I remember when I first started dating again, it was weird, I did not know what to talk about other than my children and kids' movies. You are laughing, because you are doing something or you're laughing at me either way, it is good you are laughing at this moment. When was the last time you had a good laugh? I remember signing up for a dating program and they would match me up with guys and we would meet up for lunch or dinner. There is an example of one of my dates I never looked back on however, it provided me with a laugh; During the date, the guy talked about living with his mother and going to Disney world by himself. When I asked if he had children, he said no. When the bartender brought over the check, the guy looked over at me and said he was saving up his money for his next Disney trip and wanted to know if I wanted to join him. Let me just say the date ended before it truly started. That night I laughed the entire night. I started to remember what it was like to truly laugh and how much I missed it. I went out on a few more dates. It was nice to get out and be around other adults. During this dating time I had the opportunity to get to know myself again and find out what truly makes me happy that I it is not for a person to make me happy but for me to be happy with the person I am.

The one who will make you smile and laugh the person you can be yourself around. The person who will love you for who you are, the real you. Have you ever had a talk with someone about that perfect person? I have come to realize that perfect person is the perfect person for everyone. The perfect person is out there, we all have that perfect person for each other. That perfect person was not meant to be perfect for everyone else, only perfect for the person they are meant to be with. We all have that perfect person for each one of us. Once the dating journey was over, I started reading books about self-help, personal development, and I once read a dating book. I found these books very enjoyable because it allowed me to better understand myself and build on my communication skills. During this time, I learned to accept a compliment as a compliment. Have you ever noticed when someone give us a compliment we tend to go into details? I stopped doing that and take the compliment and move forward. As I continue to grow, I learn more about myself. I understand the importance of exercising and the more I stuck to working out no less than thirty minutes per day. My attitude and my energy levels changed. I did not make these changes all overnight, it took some time to figure out what would work for me. Once I figured out how to fit it into my busy schedule, I had to learn how to stay committed. It was not easy. I would have a few days in a row and would fall off. The biggest thing to learn is that I never gave up and I pushed myself harder and harder, even on the days when I did not want to work out. I had to be my biggest fan to myself. Once that workout was over I would the feel a sense of accomplishment come over me. Restore to me the joy of your salvation and uphold me with wiling spirit. Psalm 51:12

CHAPTER 10

Laugh, Live, and Love

Sometimes it hard to find time to laugh with all the things you have going on. It is said that laughing boosts oxygen intake and helps release endorphins. I have noticed after I laugh extremely hard, I feel more relaxed. Laughter reduces the stress in your body, and after having a good laugh with a friend, have you noticed afterwards that you cannot remember why you were upset in the first place. And even if you did remember, the anger was no longer there.

Being in love is something everyone wishes and hopes for. It is so important to pay attention to what makes you happy. Sometimes you must decide to just live and live in the moment. I had to come to the realization that what I was putting out is what I would get back, so I started working on having a more positive attitude on things no matter what it is. Living in the moment and finding out what you are gifted at does not take much effort.

Though I missed the feeling of falling in love and being loved, I have learned to love myself and stay open to love. Falling in love with someone is such an exciting feeling. Being in love is such an intense feeling that takes over the relationship, the feeling of being infatuated with each other. The feeling of nervousness and giddiness when the person comes around. I am so thankful I continue to allow myself to be open to fall in love again. When you are in love you tend to see things in a different light. When you are in love, you are willing to try new things and people are more willing to come to for advice.

Even though you may not love your job, find laughter through enjoying life, a new feeling that you have not had. I had to learn to do things that made me smile such as coloring, going for a walk, and going to the movies by myself. I started attending a girl's night which I looked forward to attending. It gave me a chance to dress up and be in good company. I had to start spoiling myself, like going to get a pedicure, which is something I find very relaxing. When I was not doing things for myself, I would take the kids to the park and watch them play and just have fun.

I have learned to be grateful for what I have and not focus on what I do not have. Even with still being a single parent with no father's involved in my children's life, I still feel grateful. I am grateful I can make decisions for my children without any issues or concerns. I am grateful to be healthy and happy. I am grateful with everything I had to go through. I made it through it all and to laugh, live, and love myself. You can love you too.

FINAL THOUGHTS

As a single mom it is sometimes hard to find support when you need it. It is important to know what type of support is needed and the time it is needed. Sometimes it is difficult for a single parent to accept support when they are used to doing things by themselves. As a single parent we must pay attention to the support system we have around us. If it is hard to identify supporters, think about the activities your children participate in such as football, basketball, baseball, soccer, gymnastics, and tennis. All these activities could become your support system. Sometimes, family can be difficult, however it is important to identify the one who is supportive. You could sign up for your local neighborhood app and it can provide resources.

I identified my support systems. My oldest brother has been there for my boys. Sometimes, it is important to pay attention to the people around you because you never know who will provide additional support. Your support system are people you feel comfortable with having around your children. Your children are trusting you to make good judgment. You are your children's first role model/teachers. Being raised by a single parent I have learned to appreciate being an independent woman. Being a single parent does not make you weak or valuable, it makes you strong. It means there is nothing you cannot overcome because you have already overcome so much.

Other types of support that has helped me through this journey are the comedy movies, Vacation with Friends, Girls Trip, Central Intelligence, and Night School.